3002300045804T

S0-AIB-088

JR. GRAPHIC BIOGRAPHIES™

GEORGE WASHINGTON

and the American Revolution

Dan Abnett

PowerKiDS
press
New York

Published in 2007 by The Rosen Publishing Group, Inc.
29 East 21st Street, New York, NY 10010

Copyright © 2007 by The Rosen Publishing Group, Inc.

All rights reserved. No part of this book may be reproduced in any form without permission in writing from the publisher, except by a reviewer.

First Edition

Editors: Joanne Randolph
Book Design: Julio Gil
Illustrations: Q2A

Library of Congress Cataloging-in-Publication Data

Abnett, Dan.
  George Washington and the American Revolution / Dan Abnett.— 1st ed.
    p. cm. — (Jr. graphic biographies)
  Includes index.
  ISBN (10) 1-4042-3395-4 (13) 978-1-4042-3395-9 (lib. bdg.) —
ISBN (10) 1-4042-2148-4 (13) 978-1-4042-2148-2 (pbk.)
  1. Washington, George, 1732–1799—Juvenile literature. 2. Presidents—United
States—Biography—Juvenile literature. 3. United States—History—Revolution,
1775–1783—Juvenile literature. I. Title. II. Series. III. Graphic biographies (Rosen
Publishing Group)
  E312.66.A26 2007
  973.4'1092—dc22

                                    2005037163

Manufactured in the United States of America

CONTENTS

MAIN CHARACTERS

George Washington (1732–1799) was born in Virginia on February 22, 1732. He worked as a **surveyor** before joining the fight against the French and the Indians who fought with them in the **French and Indian War**. When the Americans rebelled against the British, Washington was chosen to lead the Army. After winning the war, he was elected as the first president of the United States.

Baron Friedrich von Steuben (1730–1794) used what he had learned in the Prussian Army to train the American soldiers during the American Revolution. The training he gave greatly improved Washington's army.

Marquis de Lafayette (1757–1854) arrived in America in June 1777. He had come to help the Americans in their fight for independence from Britain. He became very close with Washington. He also helped get the French king to provide open aid to the Americans.

Henry Clinton (1730–1795) was put in charge of the British army in America from 1778 to 1781. He took over for William Howe.

Charles Cornwallis (1738–1805) was the commander of the British army in the South, beginning in 1778. He was Clinton's second in command. His 1781 loss at Yorktown ended the major fighting of the war.

GEORGE WASHINGTON AND THE AMERICAN REVOLUTION

GEORGE WASHINGTON WAS BORN ON FEBRUARY 22, 1732.

HIS RICH FAMILY OWNED A LARGE **PLANTATION** IN VIRGINIA.

WHEN GEORGE WAS 11 YEARS OLD, HIS FATHER DIED.

GEORGE WASHINGTON DECIDED TO LEARN HOW TO SURVEY THE LAND.

IN 1749, HE BECAME THE SURVEYOR FOR CULPEPER COUNTY, VIRGINIA.

DURING A TRIP TO THE WEST INDIES IN 1750, GEORGE GOT SICK WITH **SMALLPOX**. HE LIVED.

IN 1754, THE FRENCH AND INDIAN WAR BEGAN. WASHINGTON QUICKLY BECAME COMMANDER OF THE VIRGINIA **MILITIA**.

IN 1759, WASHINGTON MARRIED MARTHA DANDRIDGE CUSTIS.

SHE CAME TO LIVE AT MOUNT VERNON, WASHINGTON'S PLANTATION.

THE FRENCH AND INDIAN WAR FINALLY ENDED IN 1763.

THE WAR HAD BEEN COSTLY AND THE BRITISH DECIDED TO TAX THE AMERICANS.

THE BRITISH TAX US, YET WE HAVE NO SAY IN GOVERNMENT. WE MUST **PROTEST!**

ON MARCH 5, 1770, A GROUP OF AMERICANS **RIOTED**. THE BRITISH TROOPS FIRED ON THE CROWD. THEY KILLED FIVE PEOPLE AND HURT SIX MORE.

THIS BECAME KNOWN AS THE BOSTON **MASSACRE**.

ON DECEMBER 16, 1773, AMERICANS DRESSED AS NATIVE AMERICANS BOARDED A BRITISH SHIP.

DUMP THE TEA INTO THE OCEAN, BOYS!

THIS WAS CALLED THE BOSTON TEA PARTY.

IN 1774, WASHINGTON ATTENDED THE FIRST CONTINENTAL CONGRESS.

WE MUST DECIDE WHAT TO DO ABOUT BRITAIN.

NOT EVERYONE AGREED ON WHAT TO DO.

WE MUST TRY TO SORT THIS OUT.

WE SHOULD PREPARE TO FIGHT!

THE AMERICANS HEARD THAT THE BRITISH PLANNED TO ATTACK CONCORD, MASSACHUSETTS.

AWAKE! TO ARMS! THE BRITISH ARMY IS COMING!

ON APRIL 18, 1775, PAUL REVERE RODE HARD TO CONCORD TO WARN THE **PATRIOTS**.

THE BRITISH TRAVELED THROUGH LEXINGTON ON THEIR WAY TO CONCORD. THEY WERE MET BY 70 MILITIAMEN. THE FIRST SHOTS OF THE AMERICAN REVOLUTION WERE FIRED.

THE AMERICAN MILITIA USED THE LAND AND THE BUILDINGS TO **PROTECT** THEMSELVES. THEY FORCED THE BRITISH BACK TO BOSTON.

THAT MAY WASHINGTON WAS CHOSEN TO LEAD THE CONTINENTAL ARMY.

I ACCEPT. I HOPE OUR **VICTORY** WILL COME QUICKLY.

A FEW MONTHS LATER THE BRITISH GOVERNMENT SENT AN ARMY TO PUT A STOP TO THE REBELLION.

GEORGE WASHINGTON KEPT THE BRITISH TROOPS UNDER **SIEGE** IN BOSTON. THEY HAD NO CHOICE BUT TO LEAVE THE CITY IN MARCH 1776.

ON JULY 4, 1776, CONGRESS SIGNED THE **DECLARATION** OF INDEPENDENCE.

WASHINGTON READ THE DECLARATION TO HIS TROOPS IN NEW YORK A FEW DAYS LATER.

WE DECLARE THAT THESE **UNITED** COLONIES ARE, AND OF RIGHT OUGHT TO BE FREE AND INDEPENDENT STATES.

LATER THAT SUMMER BRITISH TROOPS LANDED AT STATEN ISLAND, NEW YORK.

THE BRITISH FORCES THEN TOOK OVER LONG ISLAND. THEY SOON FORCED WASHINGTON'S MEN OUT OF NEW YORK.

ON CHRISTMAS NIGHT 1776, GEORGE WASHINGTON TOOK HIS TROOPS ACROSS THE DELAWARE RIVER. HE PLANNED A SURPRISE ATTACK ON TRENTON, NEW JERSEY.

HE TOOK THE TOWN, ALONG WITH 900 PRISONERS.

KEEP IT QUIET, BOYS.

WASHINGTON LEFT A FEW MEN BEHIND IN TRENTON TO FOOL THE BRITISH.

HE MOVED THE REST OF HIS ARMY TOWARD PRINCETON, NEW JERSEY.

SOON BRITISH GENERAL CORNWALLIS ARRIVED IN TRENTON.

THEY HAVE ALL GONE, SIR.

WASHINGTON CAME UNDER ATTACK OUTSIDE PRINCETON. HE GAVE HIS MEN THE **COURAGE** TO FIGHT.

LET US STAND TOGETHER, MY BRAVE FELLOWS!

SOON MORE AMERICAN TROOPS ARRIVED. THE BRITISH WERE BEATEN.

THAT SPRING THE AMERICAN FORCES **DEFENDED** PHILADELPHIA.

THEY WERE FORCED TO **RETREAT**.

ON OCTOBER 17, AT THE BATTLE OF SARATOGA, THEIR LUCK CHANGED.

THE BRITISH **SURRENDER**. THE DAY IS OURS!

WASHINGTON TOOK HIS TROOPS TO VALLEY FORGE FOR THE WINTER.

MANY MEN DIED OR LEFT THE ARMY DURING THIS LONG, HARD WINTER.

THE MEN WHO STAYED STILL HAD TO PREPARE FOR MORE FIGHTING.

BARON VON STEUBEN, I NEED YOUR SKILL TO TRAIN MY ARMY.

BY THE SPRING THE ARMY WAS BETTER THAN EVER.

MARQUIS DE LAFAYETTE, WELCOME.

THAT SAME SPRING THE FRENCH BEGAN TO HELP THE AMERICANS OPENLY.

BRITISH GENERAL HENRY CLINTON WAS ORDERED TO LEAVE PHILADELPHIA.

HE LED HIS MEN BACK TO NEW YORK.

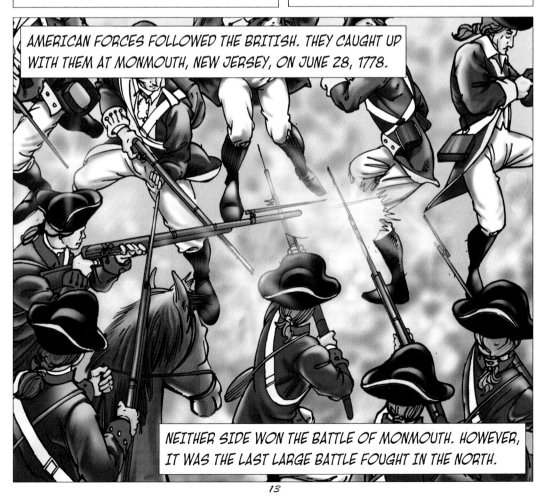

AMERICAN FORCES FOLLOWED THE BRITISH. THEY CAUGHT UP WITH THEM AT MONMOUTH, NEW JERSEY, ON JUNE 28, 1778.

NEITHER SIDE WON THE BATTLE OF MONMOUTH. HOWEVER, IT WAS THE LAST LARGE BATTLE FOUGHT IN THE NORTH.

IN JULY 1778, FRENCH SHIPS REACHED AMERICA. GEORGE WASHINGTON PLANNED TO USE THEM TO ATTACK THE BRITISH AT RHODE ISLAND.

AFTER THEY REACHED AMERICA, THE SHIPS WERE HARMED IN A HURRICANE.

THE NEXT SUMMER THE BRITISH TOOK TWO FORTS ON THE HUDSON RIVER.

GENERAL WAYNE, I WANT YOU TO ATTACK STONY POINT AND TAKE BACK THE HUDSON.

DURING THE FIGHTING GENERAL WAYNE WAS SHOT IN THE HEAD.

THANKFULLY WAYNE LIVED.

HIS MEN WENT ON TO WIN THE BATTLE AND TOOK 500 PRISONERS.

IN 1780, THE BRITISH SURROUNDED CHARLESTON, SOUTH CAROLINA.

THE AMERICANS SURRENDERED.

THINGS GOT WORSE WHEN AMERICAN TROOPS **MUTINIED** IN EARLY 1780.

THEY WERE TIRED AND HUNGRY AND THEY HAD NOT BEEN PAID.

THE BRITISH KNEW ABOUT THE MUTINY AND DECIDED TO ATTACK.

WASHINGTON'S TROOPS WERE CAMPED AT MORRISTOWN, NEW JERSEY.

THE BRITISH ARE GOING TO ATTACK US ALONG THE HUDSON RIVER. WE MUST BRING THE FIGHT TO THEM.

INSTEAD THE BRITISH MARCHED ON MORRISTOWN AFTER WASHINGTON HAD LEFT.

A SMALL NUMBER OF SOLDIERS AND TOWNSPEOPLE FORCED THE BRITISH TO RETREAT.

IN JULY 1780, THE FRENCH HAD SHIPS IN NEWPORT, RHODE ISLAND.

THE FRENCH WILL NOT ATTACK NEW YORK. IT IS TOO WELL DEFENDED BY THE BRITISH.

LAFAYETTE, I WANT YOU TO ASK THEM TO ATTACK THE BRITISH IN NEW YORK.

WASHINGTON SOON GOT MORE BAD NEWS. THE AMERICAN FORCES HAD BEEN BADLY BEATEN IN CAMDEN, SOUTH CAROLINA.

WASHINGTON HAD A HARD TIME KEEPING HIS MEN IN THE ARMY.

I KNOW YOU ARE TIRED AND HAVE NOT BEEN PAID, BUT WE NEED TO KEEP FIGHTING.

IN JANUARY 1781, MORE AMERICAN SOLDIERS MUTINIED.

THEY MARCHED TO CONGRESS TO TELL THEIR LEADERS WHY THEY WERE SO ANGRY.

CONGRESS ALLOWED MEN TO LEAVE THE ARMY. THEY ALSO SPENT MORE MONEY FEEDING AND CLOTHING THEIR SOLDIERS.

WHILE FIGHTING CONTINUED IN THE SOUTH, GEORGE WASHINGTON MET WITH GENERAL ROCHAMBEAU, COMMANDER OF THE FRENCH FORCES.

WE CAN DEFEAT HIM IF WE ACT QUICKLY.

THE MEN MADE A PLAN TO ATTACK CORNWALLIS AT YORKTOWN, VIRGINIA.

THE FRENCH WARSHIPS FIRED ON YORKTOWN FROM THE WATER.

AT THE SAME TIME, AMERICAN TROOPS SURROUNDED THE TOWN.

THE BRITISH FORCES WERE TRAPPED.

GENERAL CORNWALLIS AND THE BRITISH FORCES AT YORKTOWN SURRENDERED ON OCTOBER 19, 1781.

IN APRIL 1782, THE BRITISH AND AMERICANS BEGAN PEACE TALKS IN PARIS. THE WAR DID NOT END FOR ANOTHER YEAR, THOUGH THE MAJOR FIGHTING WAS FINISHED.

THE **TREATY** OF PARIS WAS SIGNED ON SEPTEMBER 3, 1783. THE WAR WITH THE BRITISH WAS FINALLY OVER.

THE PARIS PEACE TREATY OF 1783

IN THE NAME OF THE MOST HOLY AND UNDIVIDED TRINITY. IT HAVING PLEASED THE DIVINE PROVIDENCE TO DISPOSE THE HEARTS OF THE MOST SERENE AND MOST POTENT PRINCE GEORGE THE THIRD, BY THE GRACE OF GOD, KING OF GREAT BRITAIN, FRANCE, AND IRELAND, DEFENDER OF THE FAITH, DUKE OF BRUNSWICK AND LUNEBOURG, ARCH-TREASURER AND PRINCE ELECTOR OF THE HOLY ROMAN EMPIRE ETC., AND OF THE UNITED STATES OF AMERICA, TO FORGET ALL PAST MISUNDERSTANDINGS AND DIFFERENCES THAT HAVE UNHAPPILY INTERRUPTED THE GOOD CORRESPONDENCE AND FRIENDSHIP WHICH THEY MUTUALLY WISH TO RESTORE, AND TO ESTABLISH SUCH A BENEFICIAL AND SATISFACTORY INTERCOURSE , BETWEEN THE TWO COUNTRIES UPON THE GROUND OF RECIPROCAL ADVANTAGES AND MUTUAL CONVENIENCE AS MAY PROMOTE AND SECURE TO

WASHINGTON SPENT THE NEXT FIVE YEARS AT HOME IN MOUNT VERNON.

ON APRIL 30, 1789, GEORGE WASHINGTON WAS SWORN IN AS THE FIRST PRESIDENT OF THE UNITED STATES OF AMERICA.

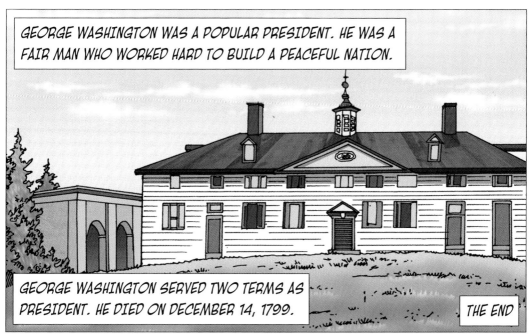

GEORGE WASHINGTON WAS A POPULAR PRESIDENT. HE WAS A FAIR MAN WHO WORKED HARD TO BUILD A PEACEFUL NATION.

GEORGE WASHINGTON SERVED TWO TERMS AS PRESIDENT. HE DIED ON DECEMBER 14, 1799.

THE END

TIMELINE

1732	George Washington is born on February 22.
1748	Washington begins to work as a surveyor.
1752	George Washington becomes the owner of Mount Vernon after his brother Lawrence dies.
1753	Washington leads a group of men to fight French claims to the Allegheny River in Virginia.
1759	Washington and Martha Dandridge Custis are married.
1773	The Boston Tea Party occurs on December 16.
1775	On April 19, the Battle of Lexington and Concord occurs.
	On June 15, Washington is made leader of the American army.
1776	The Declaration of Independence is signed on July 4.
	The war's first major battle occurs on August 20 in Long Island.
	On Christmas night, Washington and his men cross the Delaware River and attack Trenton, New Jersey.
1781	British general Cornwallis surrenders at Yorktown, Virginia, on October 19.
1783	The Treaty of Paris is signed, officially ending the war.
1789	Washington becomes the first president of the United States of America.
1799	George Washington dies at Mount Vernon.

GLOSSARY

courage (KUR-ij) Bravery.

declaration (deh-kluh-RAY-shun) An official announcement.

defended (dih-FEND-ed) Guarded from harm.

French and Indian War (FRENCH AND IN-dee-un WOR) The battles fought between 1754 and 1763 by England, France, and Native Americans for control of North America.

massacre (MA-sih-ker) The act of killing a large number of people or animals.

militia (muh-LIH-shuh) A group of people who are trained and ready to fight when needed.

mutinied (MYOO-tuh-need) Disobeyed a captain's orders.

patriots (PAY-tree-uts) American colonists who believed in separating from British rule.

plantation (plan-TAY-shun) A very large farm where crops are grown.

protect (pruh-TEKT) To keep from harm.

protest (PROH-test) To carry out an act of disagreement.

retreat (rih-TREET) To back away from a fight or another hard position.

rioted (RY-ut-ed) To have been disorderly and out of control.

siege (SEEJ) Blocking off a fort or a city with soldiers so that nothing can get in or go out.

smallpox (SMOL-poks) An often deadly sickness that leaves marks on the skin.

surrender (suh-REN-der) To give up.

surveyor (ser-VAY-er) Someone who measures land.

treaty (TREE-tee) An official agreement, signed and agreed upon by each party.

united (yoo-NYT-ed) Brought together to act as a single group.

victory (VIK-tuh-ree) The winning of a battle or contest.

INDEX

WEB SITES

Due to the changing nature of Internet links, the Rosen Publishing Group, Inc., has developed an online list of Web sites related to the subject of this book. This site is updated regularly. Please use this link to access the list:
www.powerkidslinks.com/jgb/gwashing/